# VIKINGS

## SCANDINAVIA'S FEROCIOUS SEA RAIDERS

By Nel Yomtov
Illustrated by Silvio dB

raintree
a Capstone company — publishers for children

Raintree is an imprint of Capstone Global Library Limited, a company incorporated in England and Wales having its registered office at 264 Banbury Road, Oxford, OX2 7DY – Registered company number: 6695582

www.raintree.co.uk
myorders@raintree.co.uk

Edited by Aaron J. Sautter
Designed by Ted Williams and Nathan Gassman
Original illustrations © Capstone Global Library Limited 2020
Picture research by Jo Miller
Production by Kathy McColley
Originated by Capstone Global Library Ltd
Printed and bound in India

ISBN 978 I 4747 8176 3 (hardback)
ISBN 978 I 4747 6862 7 (paperback)

**British Library Cataloguing in Publication Data**
A full catalogue record for this book is available from the British Library.

**Acknowledgements**
We would like to thank the following for permission to reproduce design elements:
Shutterstock: Reinhold Leitner

# CONTENTS

# WHO WERE THE VIKINGS?

In the late 700s, the Vikings lived in Scandinavian countries, including Denmark, Sweden, Norway and parts of Finland.

Most Vikings lived in small towns along rivers or the sea. They made their living mainly as farmers, craftsmen and fishermen.

Vikings were skilled blacksmiths. They forged iron into many dangerous weapons, helmets and armour.

Male Vikings were required to own weapons, and they were always armed.

That is a fine sword. Is it true you sleep with it by your side?

Ha! No, but I hang it by my bed every night!

These weapons will be useful for our next voyage. The chieftain will enjoy this new sword. I'll decorate its handle with silver and gold.

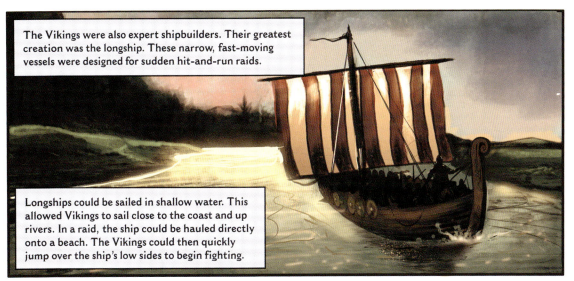

The Vikings were also expert shipbuilders. Their greatest creation was the longship. These narrow, fast-moving vessels were designed for sudden hit-and-run raids.

Longships could be sailed in shallow water. This allowed Vikings to sail close to the coast and up rivers. In a raid, the ship could be hauled directly onto a beach. The Vikings could then quickly jump over the ship's low sides to begin fighting.

Land ahead! Odin has blessed our journey!

The longship opened up a world of exploration for the Vikings. From about AD 790 to 1066, they journeyed far and wide to conquer new lands.

We beg you . . . please, spare our lives!

Show them no mercy!

Driven by a thirst for land and riches, the Vikings raided hundreds of towns and villages throughout Europe. They usually struck suddenly and without warning. The attacks were ruthless and bloody. The Vikings' hunger for treasure was boundless . . .

5

Three ships approach. They must be traders heading for the mainland.

But . . . no. They come straight towards the island. What strange ships they are!

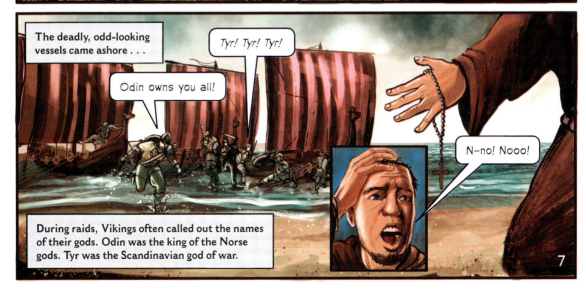

The deadly, odd-looking vessels came ashore . . .

Tyr! Tyr! Tyr!

Odin owns you all!

N–no! Nooo!

During raids, Vikings often called out the names of their gods. Odin was the king of the Norse gods. Tyr was the Scandinavian god of war.

The monks in the village saw the attack on their brother. Panicked and fearful, they tried to hide from the raiders.

But there was nowhere to hide. Within minutes, the attackers found their prey.

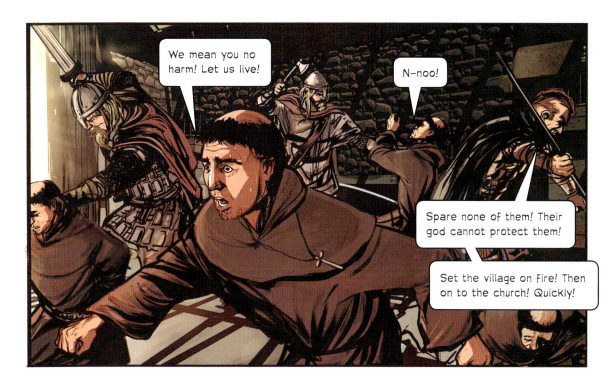

The Vikings carried off monks and pilgrims in chains. They took the prisoners back to Scandinavia as slaves.

Noo! Have mercy!

Let me go!

The victims never returned to their homeland.

The violence of the attack and looting of the church shocked the local people.

The invaders were pagans and believed in many gods. The locals believed the Vikings' raid to be an attack on Christianity itself.

The savage attack on Lindisfarne was only the beginning. The raid marked the start of 300 years of Viking pillaging.

Over time, the Vikings plundered the British Isles and most of Europe. Their raids ranged as far east as Russia and south to the Mediterranean Sea.

The invaders from Scandinavia seemed unstoppable.

ICELAND

Atlantic Ocean

IRELAND

SCANDINAVIA

North Sea

RUSSIA

BRITAIN

POLAND

GERMANY

FRANCE

HUNGARY

SPAIN

Mediterranean Sea

# TAKING EUROPE BY STORM

For the next 50 years, the Vikings targeted mainly churches and monasteries throughout the British Isles.

These people believe we attack because we oppose Christianity and their god.

Not so! We attack because they are weak and easily defeated!

By the 830s, Vikings were spending winters in the lands they raided. They established winter camps, and then launched new attacks in the spring.

In AD 841 Norwegian Vikings wintered in Ireland for the first time. They founded the city of Dublin, the present-day capital of Ireland.

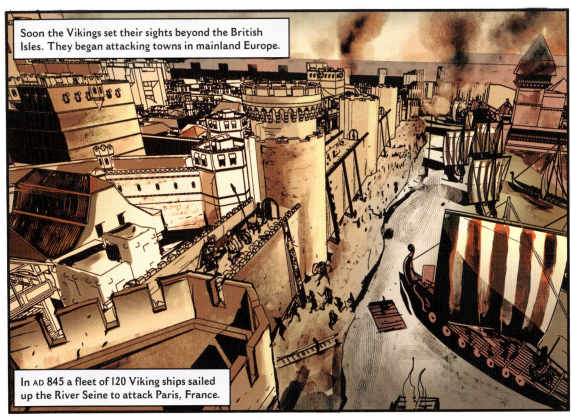

Soon the Vikings set their sights beyond the British Isles. They began attacking towns in mainland Europe.

In AD 845 a fleet of 120 Viking ships sailed up the River Seine to attack Paris, France.

The Danish Viking Ragnar Lodbrok led the raid. Thousands of Viking warriors crushed the army of King Charles the Bald.

Seven thousand pounds of gold and silver are a small price to pay for your city — and your life.

Ragnar returned to Denmark a wealthy man. But the Vikings continued to raid Paris for the next 40 years.

In time the Vikings were no longer satisfied with waging small hit-and-run raids. They wanted to conquer and control other lands.

In AD 865 the Great Viking Army invaded Anglo-Saxon Britain. The army was a union of warriors from each Scandinavian country.

Among the army's leaders were three of Ragnar Lodbrok's sons – Ivar the Boneless, Halfdan and Ubbe.

This land shall be ours, brothers!

GRRAAA!!

Fight as you never have before!

During the years of fighting, Vikings seized control of many regions of Britain. Finally in AD 878, Anglo-Saxon warriors defeated the Vikings in the south.

However, the Vikings held control of northern and eastern England for many years.

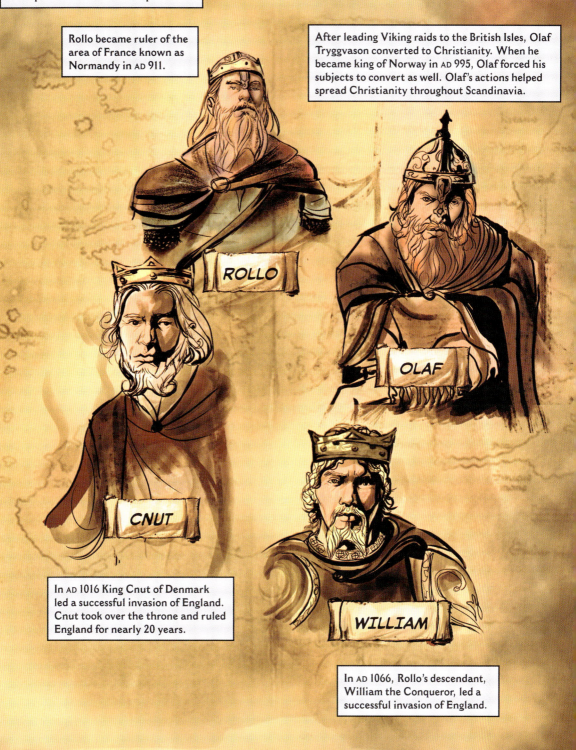

For the next 200 years, the Vikings had widespread influence in Europe.

Rollo became ruler of the area of France known as Normandy in AD 911.

After leading Viking raids to the British Isles, Olaf Tryggvason converted to Christianity. When he became king of Norway in AD 995, Olaf forced his subjects to convert as well. Olaf's actions helped spread Christianity throughout Scandinavia.

ROLLO

OLAF

CNUT

WILLIAM

In AD 1016 King Cnut of Denmark led a successful invasion of England. Cnut took over the throne and ruled England for nearly 20 years.

In AD 1066, Rollo's descendant, William the Conqueror, led a successful invasion of England.

# FATHER AND SON EXPLORERS

Along with raiding and conquering parts of Europe, the Vikings were eager to explore and find new lands. By AD 870 the Scandinavians had settled on a new island they called Iceland.

But by the middle of the 900s, Iceland was full of people and running out of space.

Soon all the good farmland will be taken.

The time has come to break new ground elsewhere.

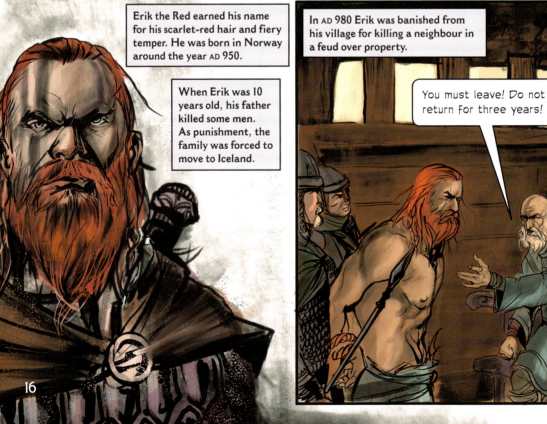

Erik the Red earned his name for his scarlet-red hair and fiery temper. He was born in Norway around the year AD 950.

When Erik was 10 years old, his father killed some men. As punishment, the family was forced to move to Iceland.

In AD 980 Erik was banished from his village for killing a neighbour in a feud over property.

You must leave! Do not return for three years!

In AD 982 Erik assembled a crew and sailed west from Iceland. He sailed in search of a mysterious land he'd heard about from earlier Viking sailors.

Finally, after sailing more than 1,600 kilometres (1,000 miles) . . .

The tales were true! Prepare to go ashore and explore!

Magnificent! These walls of ice rise from the very sea!

Erik and his men explored the enormous island for the next three years. On the west coast he found land fit to live on.

The land here looks good to farm and keep livestock.

The winters have been harsh, but our people are used to the snow and cold winds.

Perhaps we can get others to join us.

When he returned to Iceland, Erik told others about the new land he had discovered. He called it "Greenland", hoping that people would be eager to go if it had an attractive name.

The land is beautiful and the farming is good! Besides, all the good land in Iceland is taken.

I'll return with you, Erik!

As will I. We can start a new life in this new world!

Erik's encouraging words convinced many people that Greenland held great promise. In AD 986 he led a fleet of 25 ships and 400 settlers to the new land. Only 14 ships completed the voyage, but soon other settlers followed.

We'll survive these storms and arrive in two days!

A land of opportunity awaits us!

The same year Erik the Red settled in Greenland, a Viking merchant called Bjarni attempted to sail there from Iceland. But after getting lost in a thick fog, he found a new land instead.

Is it Greenland, Bjarni?

I don't think so. This land has no mountains, and it is covered with thick forests. We won't land here. Continue sailing on.

When he reached Greenland, Bjarni told others his unusual story.

One Greenlander intrigued by Bjarni's story was Leif Erikson, the son of Erik the Red.

I want to buy your ship, Bjarni. I plan to find the land you saw.

May the gods be with you. Good luck.

In about the year AD 1000, Leif sailed west from Greenland with a crew of 35 men. First they came upon a desolate, barren land.

I name this place Helluland for all the flat stones on shore.

*Hella* means "flat rocks" in the Old Norse language.

Sailing south, the men found land with sandy beaches and dense woods.

This shall be called Markland because of its thick forests.

*Markland* means "forest land" in Old Norse.

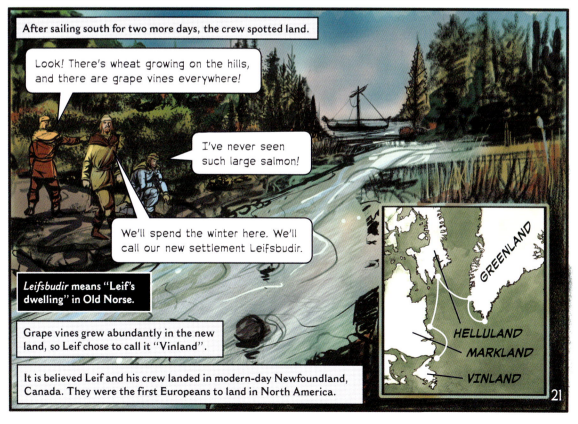

After sailing south for two more days, the crew spotted land.

Look! There's wheat growing on the hills, and there are grape vines everywhere!

I've never seen such large salmon!

We'll spend the winter here. We'll call our new settlement Leifsbudir.

*Leifsbudir* means "Leif's dwelling" in Old Norse.

Grape vines grew abundantly in the new land, so Leif chose to call it "Vinland".

It is believed Leif and his crew landed in modern-day Newfoundland, Canada. They were the first Europeans to land in North America.

GREENLAND

HELLULAND
MARKLAND
VINLAND

Many Inuits returned to seek revenge on the invaders.

Thorvald's been hit!

H–he's dead!

Many lives were lost in the fighting. Thorvald's settlers remained in Vinland until the following spring and then returned to Greenland.

In the years that followed, few Vikings returned to North America. None established lasting colonies.

The Vikings never ventured further west than Vinland. The great age of Viking exploration had ended.

23

# THE END OF AN ERA

By the mid-1000s the Vikings' power had begun to weaken. The spread of Christianity was an important reason for their decline. Many Vikings who settled in Europe became Christians like the local people.

We accept our new faith and agree to live in peace with our fellow Christians.

It shall be done.

Other Vikings brought Christianity back to Scandinavia when they returned home.

Yet Norway's Harald Hardrada still hungered for power and conquest. Harald had led raids throughout Eastern Europe, Turkey, the Middle East and the Mediterranean. Harald's success made him a wealthy man. By the 1050s he returned to Scandinavia, ready to strike again.

I have long desired the throne of England . . . it shall be my next target!

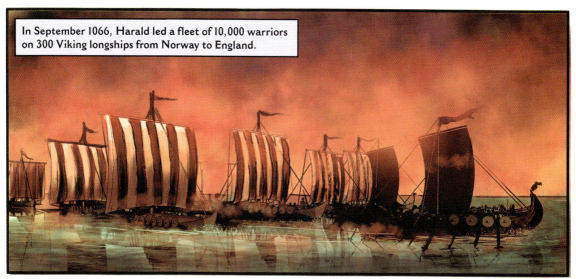

In September 1066, Harald led a fleet of 10,000 warriors on 300 Viking longships from Norway to England.

On 20 September Harald's forces crushed an English army at the Battle of Fulford. The English leaders agreed to accept Harald as their new king and turn over hostages they had captured.

An account of the battle claimed Harald had *"made such a severe onslaught that everything gave way before him"*.

Set up camp at Stamford Bridge to the north. The English will bring the hostages they captured to us there.

Stamford Bridge. 25 September 1066. The hostages never arrived . . .

What?! An English army! Grab your weapons and form a defensive circle! Quickly!

25

The fierce fighting at Stamford raged for hours. Then . . .

Yee—aggh!

Harald's been struck by an arrow!

Pursue them! Not a single one shall live!

Our leader is dead! Retreat!

Few Vikings survived the battle. Only 24 out of 300 Viking longships returned to Norway.

Harald Hardrada is often called "The Last Great Viking". His defeat at Stamford Bridge marked the end of the Viking era. After 300 years of raids and pillaging, the Vikings were no longer a force to be feared in Europe.

The Vikings left behind a rich legacy. They developed advanced shipbuilding techniques. Their longships allowed them to travel further by sea than anyone before.

Scandinavian words and phrases found their way into the English language. Over time, Old Norse words such as *deyja*, *hreindyri* and *Thorsdagr* became "die", "reindeer" and "Thursday" in English.

The Vikings also founded major European cities, such as Dublin in Ireland. They were the first to colonize the Shetland Islands and the Orkney Islands off the northern coast of Scotland.

Today millions of Europeans are direct descendants of the Vikings – perhaps the greatest warriors of all time.

27

# MORE ABOUT VIKINGS

## RAIDERS AND EXPLORERS OF EUROPE

**1**    **793**

Vikings raid Lindisfarne church and monastery. Many monks are killed and the Vikings take much treasure and many captives.

**4**    **865-878**

Led by the sons of Ragnar Lodbrok, the Great Viking Army attacks and conquers much of northern and eastern England.

**6**    **1000**

Leif Erikson sails west to North America. He discovers a region rich with food and good land. Leif names it Vinland and builds a small settlement there.

**8**    **1066**

At the Battle of Stamford Bridge, Harald Hardrada, the "Last Great Viking", is killed and his army defeated.

**840-841**

Vikings establish bases in Ireland and found the city of Dublin.

**845**

Ragnar Lodbrok leads attack on Paris, France, capturing the city and a large treasure of silver and gold.

**986**

Erik the Red establishes new colonies on Greenland.

**1004**

Led by Leif Erikson's brother Thorvald, a small group of Vikings are attacked by Inuits in Vinland. Thorvald is killed in the encounter. The Vikings leave North America the following spring.

**2**   **3**      **5**      **7**

# THE TOOLS OF WAR

As skilled metalworkers, Vikings were capable of making high-quality weapons. The major offensive weapons used by Vikings were the sword, axe and spear.

## DOUBLE-EDGED SWORD

The double-edged sword measured about 1 metre (3 feet) long. The points of the swords were generally dull. The weapons were designed more for cutting than stabbing.

## BATTLE-AXE

The battle-axe featured broad blades and was used with two hands.

## SPEARS

The Vikings used two main types of spear: a heavy spear that was thrown and a lighter thrusting spear. Both types had wooden shafts.

# GLOSSARY

**chieftain** leader of a tribe or clan of people

**convert** change from one religion or faith to another

**descendants** people who can trace their family roots back to a person or people who lived long ago

**hostage** person taken by force and held against his or her will, often as a way to demand something for their safe return

**livestock** animals kept on a farm, such as sheep, pigs and cows

**monastery** building or group of buildings where monks live, work and study their religious beliefs

**monk** man who lives in a religious community and promises to devote his life to his religion

**onslaught** fierce or destructive attack

**pagan** person who may worship many gods or none at all

**pilgrim** person who travels to a holy place, for religious reasons

**pillage** steal money or goods using violence

**plunder** steal things by force, often during battle

**ruthless** cruel and without pity for others

**trove** collection of money or other valuable objects

# FIND OUT MORE

*DKfindout! Vikings,* Philip Steele (DK Children, 2018)

*Norse Myths and Legends* (All About Myths), Anita Ganeri (Raintree, 2015)

*The Viking and Anglo-Saxon Struggle for England* (Early British History), Claire Throp (Raintree, 2016)

*The Viking Express* (Newspapers from History), Andrew Langley (Raintree, 2018)

———

# COMPREHENSION QUESTIONS

- Imagine you are the leader of a medieval village or town. What would you do to defend it from a Viking attack?

- Use other books or the internet to research ninjas and samurai warriors. Describe how their armour, weapons and combat methods were different from the Vikings.

- In your opinion, were Vikings more successful as raiders or as explorers? Explain your answer.

# INDEX

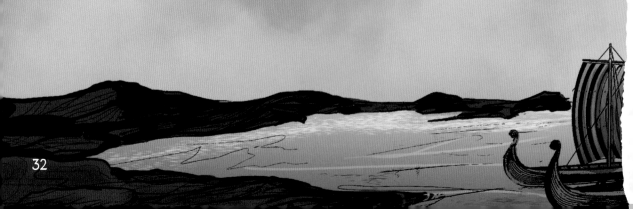